KINDERGARTEN WRITING WORKBOOK

This book belongs to:

_____

Copyright © 2023 Lucas & Friends by RV AppStudios

Fun activities

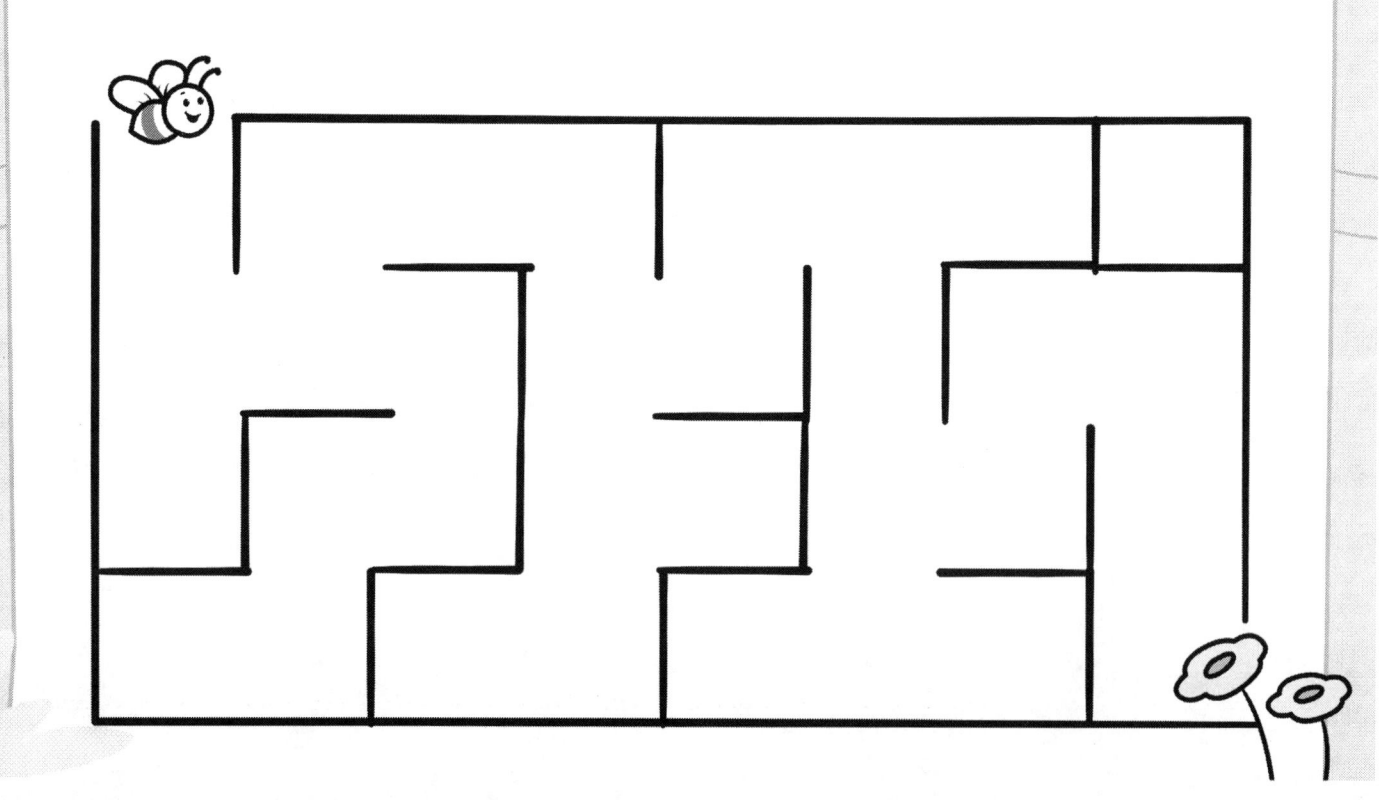

	5					
4	+	1	=			
	3				3	
	=				+	
		+	4	=	12	
					=	
	20	-		=	15	

Find and circle 6 differences

Connect the dots and color it

Color the picture

Color the picture

Made in the USA
Middletown, DE
11 July 2025